ANDRÉ PREVIN

THE GIRAFFES GO TO HAMBURG

for Soprano, Alto Flute and Piano

text by Isak Dinesen

ED 4137

first printing: April 2001

ISBN 0-634-01654-7

G. SCHIRMER, Inc.

DISTRIBUTED BY
HAL•LEONARD®
CORPORATION
7777 W. BLUEMOUND RD. P.C. BOX 13819 MILWAUKEE, WI 53213

IN THE harbor of Mombasa lay a rusty German cargo steamer, homeward bound. Upon the deck there stood a tall wooden case, and above the edge of the case rose the heads of two Giraffes. They were going to Hamburg, to a traveling Menagerie.

The Giraffes turned their delicate heads from the one side to the other, as if they were surprised, which they might well be. They had not seen the Sea before. They could only just have room to stand in the narrow case. The world had suddenly shrunk, changed and closed round them.

They could not know or imagine the degradation to which they were sailing. For they were proud and innocent creatures, gentle amblers of the great plains; they had not the least knowledge of captivity, cold, stench, smoke, and mange, nor of the terrible boredom in a world in which nothing is ever happening.

Crowds will be coming in from the wind and sleet of the streets to gaze on the Giraffes. They will point and laugh at the long slim necks when the graceful, patient, smoky-eyed heads are raised over the railings of the menagerie; they look much too long in there. The children will be frightened at the sight and cry, or they will fall in love with the Giraffes, and hand them bread. Then the fathers and mothers will think the Giraffes nice beasts, and believe that they are giving them a good time.

In the long years before them, will the Giraffes sometimes dream of their lost country? Where are they now, where have they gone to, the grass and the thorn-trees, the rivers and water-holes and the blue mountains? The high sweet air over the plains has lifted and withdrawn. Where have the other Giraffes gone to, that were side by side with them when they set going, and cantered over the undulating land? They have left them, they have all gone, and it seems that they are never coming back.

In the night where is the full moon?

Good-bye, good-bye, I wish for you that you may die on the journey, both of you, so that not one of the little noble heads, that are now raised, surprised, over the edge of the case, against the blue sky of Mombasa, shall be left to turn from one side to the other, all alone, in Hamburg, where no one knows of Africa.

The Giraffes Go to Hamburg
*was first performed on May 3, 2000
at the New Jersey Performing Arts Center, Newark,
by Renée Fleming, soprano, with
André Previn, piano, and Renée Siebert, alto flute*

recording available on CD
Deutsche Grammophon 471 028-2

duration: ca. 12 minutes

for Mia

THE GIRAFFES GO TO HAMBURG

Isak Dinesen

André Previn

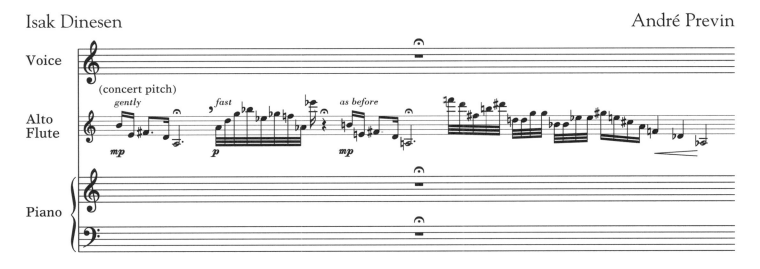

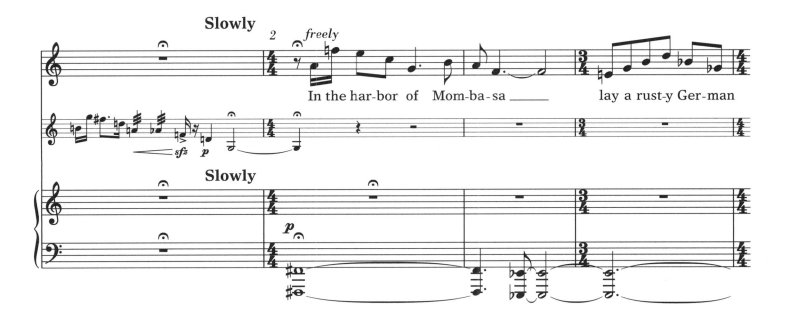

Up-on the deck there stood a tall wood-en case, and a - bove the edge of the case rose the heads of two

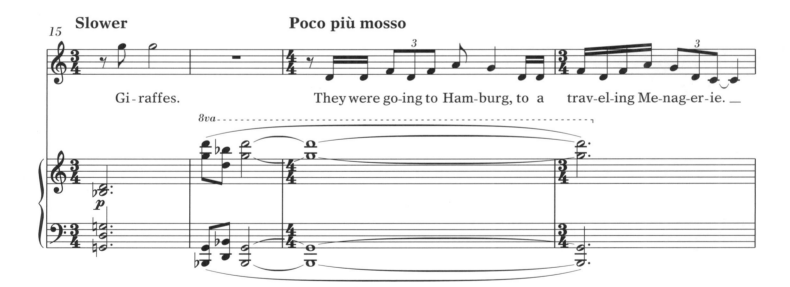

Slower   **Poco più mosso**

Gi - raffes.   They were go-ing to Ham-burg, to a trav-el-ing Me-nag-er-ie. _

Moderato

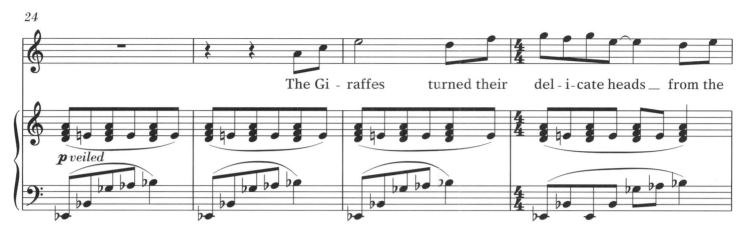

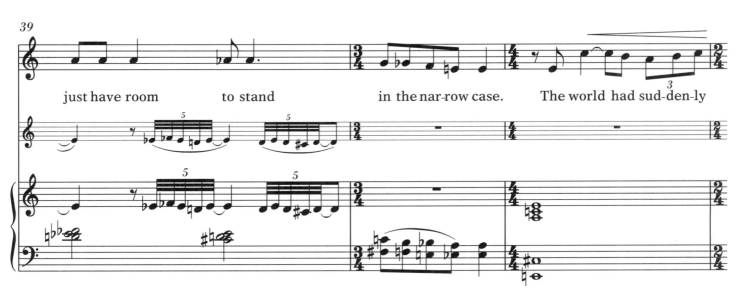

just have room   to stand   in the nar-row case.   The world had sud-den-ly

shrunk,   changed and   closed round them. ＿

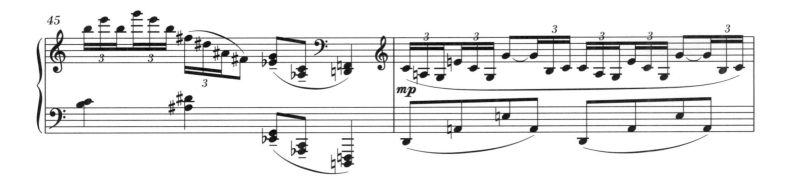

They   could not   know ＿＿＿＿＿ or im - ag - ine   the

nor of the ter-ri-ble

bore-dom in a world in which noth-ing is ev - er hap-pen-ing. _

Crowds will be com - ing in from the wind and sleet of the streets to

ANDRÉ PREVIN

THE GIRAFFES GO TO HAMBURG

for Soprano, Alto Flute and Piano

text by Isak Dinesen

Alto Flute

G. SCHIRMER, Inc.

DISTRIBUTED BY

HAL•LEONARD®
CORPORATION
7777 W. BLUEMOUND RD. P.O. BOX 13819 MILWAUKEE, WI 53213

ALTO FLUTE

for Mia

THE GIRAFFES GO TO HAMBURG

Isak Dinesen

André Previn

Voice

"as if they were sur-prised, which they might well be."

Voice

"They could on-ly just have room to stand"

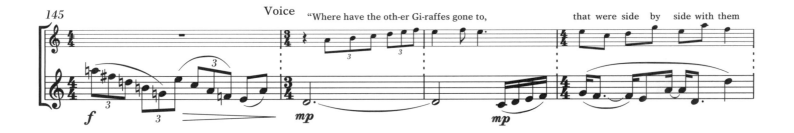

gaze on — the Gi - raffes.

They will point — and laugh at the long slim necks when the

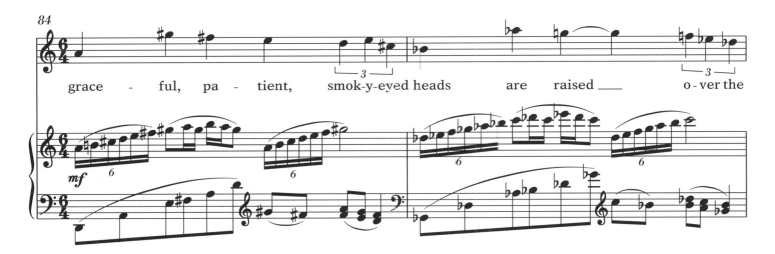

grace - ful, pa - tient, smok-y-eyed heads are raised — o - ver the

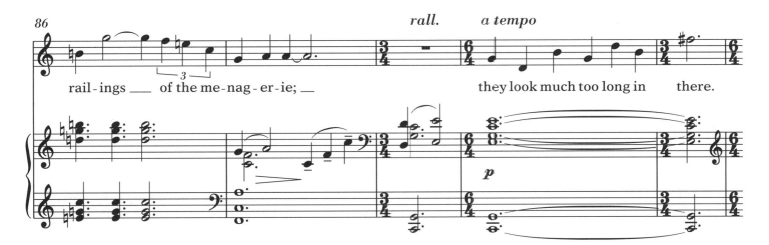

rail-ings — of the me-nag-er-ie; — they look much too long in there.

The chil-dren will be fright-ened at the sight ___
___ and cry, or they will fall in love with the Gi - raffes, ___
___ and hand them bread.

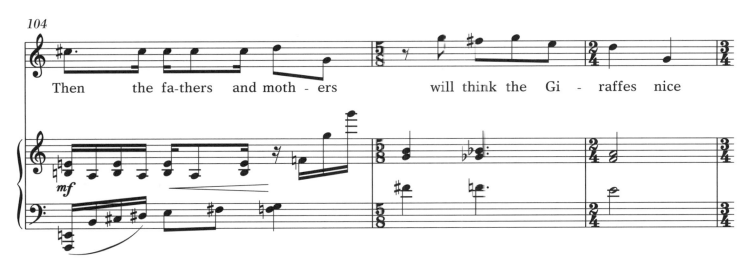

Then the fa-thers and moth - ers will think the Gi - raffes nice

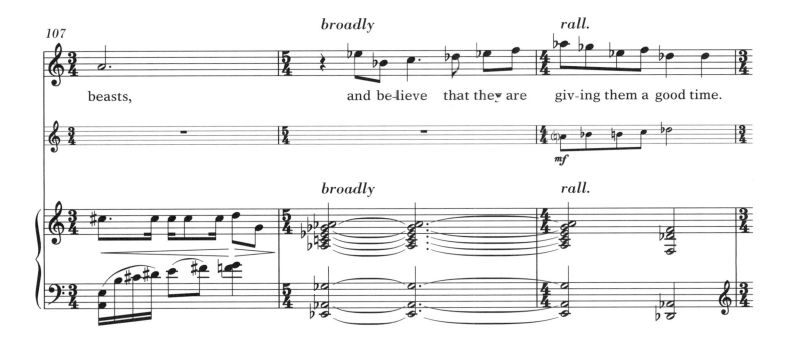

broadly *rall.*

beasts, and be-lieve that they are giv-ing them a good time.

broadly *rall.*

as before *sadly*

In the long

as before

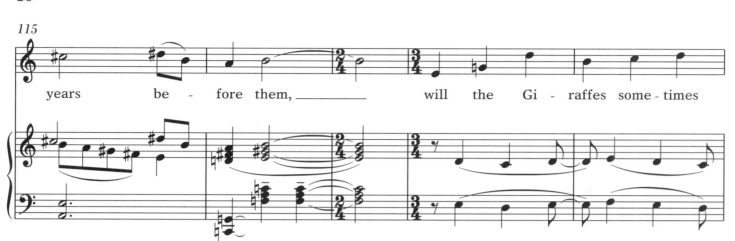

years be - fore them, _____ will the Gi - raffes some - times

dream of their lost coun - try? _____

urgent

Where are they now, where have they gone to,

the grass and the thorn - trees, the riv - ers and wa - ter - holes

Slowly

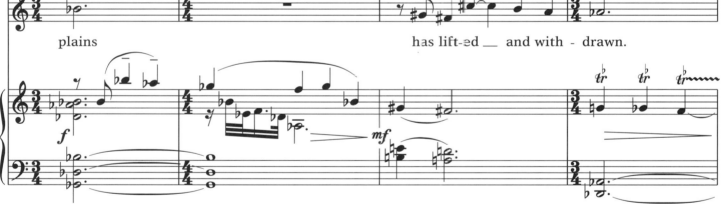

and the blue ____ moun - tains? The high sweet air o - ver the

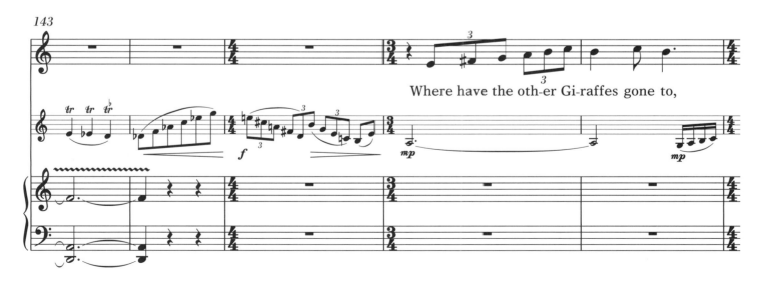

plains

has lift - ed ____ and with - drawn.

Where have the oth - er Gi - raffes gone to,

148

that were side by side with them when they set go-ing, and can-tered o-ver the

151

un-du-lat-ing land? They have left them, they have all gone, and it seems that they are

154

nev-er com-ing back. In the night where is the full moon?

o - ver the edge of the case, a - gainst the blue sky of Mom - ba - sa,

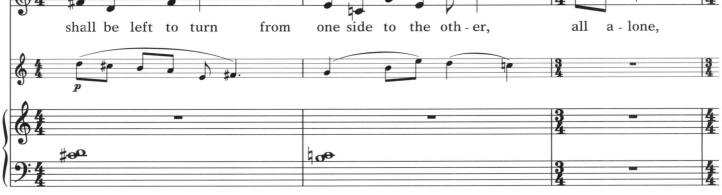

shall be left to turn from one side to the oth - er, all a - lone,

in Ham - burg, _ where no one knows of Af - ri - ca.